MEL BAY PRESENTS

JUST JAZZ GUITAR

ARTICLES

BY JACK WILKINS

Cover photo © Brian Kelly. Taken in performance at Dreamcatcher Guitars.

Jack Wilkins endorses Benedetto Archtop Guitars, DiCarlo Nylon String Guitars, LaBella Guitar Strings, Acoustic Image Amps and Raezer's Edge Speakers.

1 2 3 4 5 6 7 8 9 0

Visit us on the Web at www.melbay.com — E-mail us at email@melbay.com

TABLE OF CONTENTS

INTRODUCTION

It is with great pleasure Mel Bay Publications, Inc. releases this book by guitar legend Jack Wilkins. Jack's skills as a session player, jazz player and all around guitar virtuoso have been honed by playing countless gigs and recording sessions. This book compiles many of Jack's lessons originally written for *Just Jazz Guitar* magazine. Subjects including comping, harmonization, and single-note soloing in the jazz setting are covered in this text by one of the world's greatest... so practice hard. The material is tried and tested and will make you a better player.

Even if the material in this book is a little challenging, Mel Bay Publications and Jack Wilkins can't be held liable for any hair loss, weight gain, sexual side effects, insomnia, blurred vision, chronic fatigue, freckle and mole increase, sore throat, cellulite, rashes, hives, nausea, diarrhea, hacking cough, marital stress and sore fingers that are caused by practicing the material in this book.

These articles are grouped in a learning sequence, not chronologically.

LEARNING HOW TO PRACTICE

by Jack Wilkins

One of the most important things a student needs to learn is how to make proper use of practice time if he or she wants to develop quickly into a better player. I have to admit I spent a lot of years learning how and what to practice, and I now feel that if a student cooperates by working hard and practicing regularly. I can help them make great strides in their playing just by teaching them how to practice.

Let's take a look at the process.

A)   The most important thing a student needs to do is to be honest about how much time a day can be devoted to practicing. It's no use spending hours on one day and doing very little for the rest of the time. A little and often is the best way. Be consistent.

B)   Once you know how much time you have to devote to practicing every day, the next step is to write out a schedule and stick to it as much as possible.

What should this schedule consist of? Again honesty is invaluable in assessing and recognizing your weak points so that you can work on strengthening them.

For example, if you don't know the scale tone chords in every key, you should practice them as part of your daily schedule until you have the exercise mastered.

Here is a list of basic fundamentals that every guitarist should know:
1.   Scales – major and minor. Six basic fingerings – all keys (See Aug. '96 JJG issue)
2.   Arpeggios – 7^{ths}, extensions – all keys (See Nov. '96 JJG issue)
3.   7th chords and inversions – all keys
4.   Scale tone chords – major and minor – all keys
5.   "Rhythm" changes – all keys
6.   Blues changes – all keys
7.   Picking techniques (Aug. '97 JJG issue)
8.   Modes – major and minor – all keys
9.   Inner voices (Feb. '98 JJG issue)
10.   Walking bass
11.   Reading skills
12.   Chords in 4^{ths}
13.   Intros and endings (May '98, Aug. '98, Nov. '98, Feb. '99 JJG issues)
14.   Ear training – transcribing
15.   Approach notes (Feb. 2001)
16.   Experimentation, creativity, and improvising

There are other essentials such as jam sessions, listening to lots of music and building a "musical vocabulary", reading about music and talking about it with friends and teachers and so forth.

This list may seem vast, and certainly daunting, but with a steady schedule devoted to a task, you will make great progress.

Here's a sample schedule with two hours of practice a day for a student who is just starting out:
1. Scales – major and minor, 3 or 4 keys (15 minutes)
2. Arpeggios, 7^{ths} (15 minutes)
3. Scale tone chords, 3 or 4 keys (15 minutes)
4. "Rhythm" changes. Learn the changes by heart and improvise using scales and arpeggios. (15 minutes)
5. Blues changes. Same as no. 4 (15 minutes)
6. Picking techniques (15 minutes)
7. Inner voice training (15 minutes)
8. Ear training, transcribing, tune playing, analysing harmonic structures (15 minutes)
    (Some time devoted to reading couldn't hurt!)

Of course this is just a sample list so you should revise it to suit your own needs and weaknesses. If you can devote more than two hours, all the better. Keep in mind that you should practice slowly and methodically at first, gradually building up speed as your control improves.

A metronome can be extremely helpful. Don't force yourself to do things, but feel free to take short breaks. There's no point in either straining muscles or creating "head" problems with certain exercises you're having trouble mastering.

There's no easy way to become a good player/musician. It takes work and discipline, but practicing the right things is critical to a student's steady development.

I hope some of these ideas will help make it more fun for you and give you a better focus. Good practicing!

"COMPING" PART 1

I'd like to give you some of my thoughts and feelings about "comping" (accompaniment). Having played in just about every conceivable musical situation, I feel qualified to share my experience with you. The guitar as a comping instrument is oftentimes confusing and is generally an overlooked and underrated aspect in playing jazz. There are many situations that arise where there are no clear-cut rules to follow. I'm sure you have had to play with two guitars or bass and guitar. Perhaps a big band or just you and a singer. Do you play the same for each situation? There is little doubt you have to adjust to each gig. There is an element however that is common to every playing situation. That is the desire to make the music work! All that means is comping with steady time, no slowing down or speeding up (common comping flaws), listen to the soloist and help them to finish their thoughts, not interfere with random chords and rhythmic confusion, and earn the respect of the soloist. Comping and helping are synonymous! It also means being sensitive to the overall musical picture. To be able to sense when the music is working and when it's not. I know that many players have little or no regard for dynamics, interplay, interaction with the soloist, or letting the music flow. One gets the sense that some players feel that comping is nothing more than being a second-class citizen! "Let's get this over with so I can play my s---" Nothing is further from the truth. In the 20^S and 30^S, no one comped better than Eddie Lang with Lonnie Johnson or Joe Venuti. Unbelievable, especially for it's time. Listen to Bill Evans and Jim Hall, or Herbie Hancock and how they weave there comping to suit the soloist. Their comping is highly important to the complete musical picture. Tal's recordings with Eddie Costa and Vinnie Burke are amazing! Not just Tal's single lines but the way he comped for the piano. Without drums in this trio, Tal could make his guitar sound like a snare drum! Listen to Barney with Julie London for some captivating comping. Joe Pass and Ella as well. The list is very extensive. You might say that to be an accomplished "comper", you have to listen with three ears. One, to the soloist, two, yourself, three, the whole musical scope. For the next several issues, I'll talk about specific situations and demystify some of what goes on with this wondrous art form. For now, imagine someone like Freddie Hubbard or Eric Dolphy and how you would comp for them. Until next time.

"COMPING" PART 2

In this second part of the "comping" discussion, I'd like to talk about the basic "4" to the bar rhythm which is usually the least complicated and often times the most fun. You've all heard Freddie Green with the Count Basie Band and his enormous drive that propelled the whole band to swing harder. Those old archtop guitars were usually set up with very high action to get the best possible sound and crispness. Freddie must have had hands of steel to play like that for over forty years! This "4" to the bar was also done by many other guitarists of the era including Eddie Lang, who elevated this technique to a high art form. Django's Hot Club bands played in that style and today's Gypsy jazz guitarists play in a similar fashion.

This "4" to the bar is usually played with all down strokes to get the strongest rhythmic feel. The voicings used can be quite varied but the guitarists in the early big bands usually played a three-note voicing, commonly on the 6th, 4th and 3rd strings with the other strings muted. There were, of course, other voicings but for our proposes here I'd like to give you as simple a way of becoming acquainted with this technique.

Let's look at the voicings before we approach the rhythm. Here is a G major7 with the root (G note) in the bass and its relative chords.

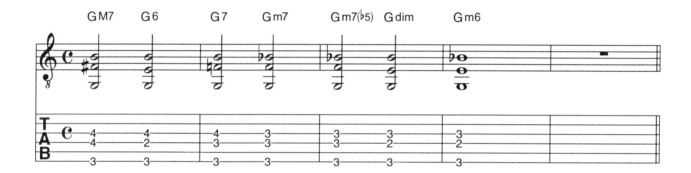

You'll notice that these voicings, lack the 5th of the chord (in this case, there is no D note in the G chord). Here's an exercise using these voicings.

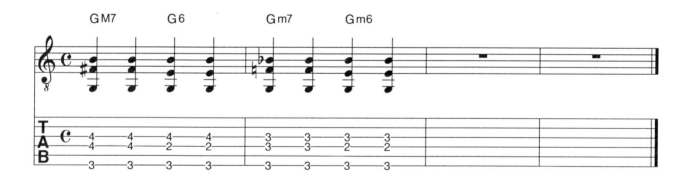

Now let's talk about the feel of this "4" to the bar rhythm. While you're playing these shapes, mute the other strings and give it a more staccato approach. After striking the chord, mute **all** the strings before the next chord is struck. The pick hand usually plays all down strokes. Here are the 1st inversions of the previous chords using the same strings – 6th, 4th and 3rd.

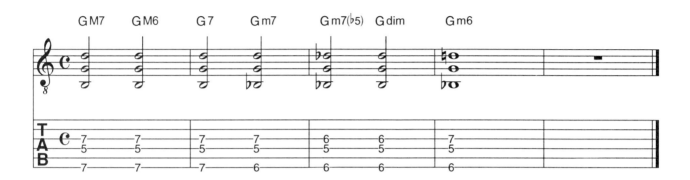

You'll notice that the GM7, GM6 and G7 are all the same voicings. That's because the 7th of the chord is missing. These chords are used more as rhythm than true harmony. Here are the 2nd inversions.

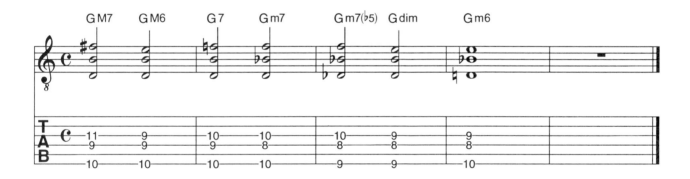

The 3rd inversion chords are a bit strange sounding having the 7th in the bass but why not check them out.

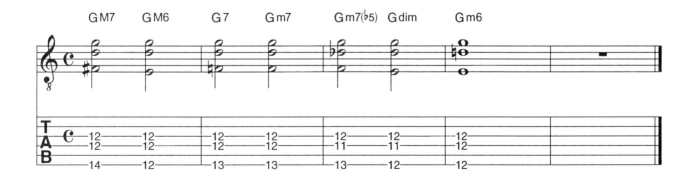

Here's an exercise using these chords and their inversions.

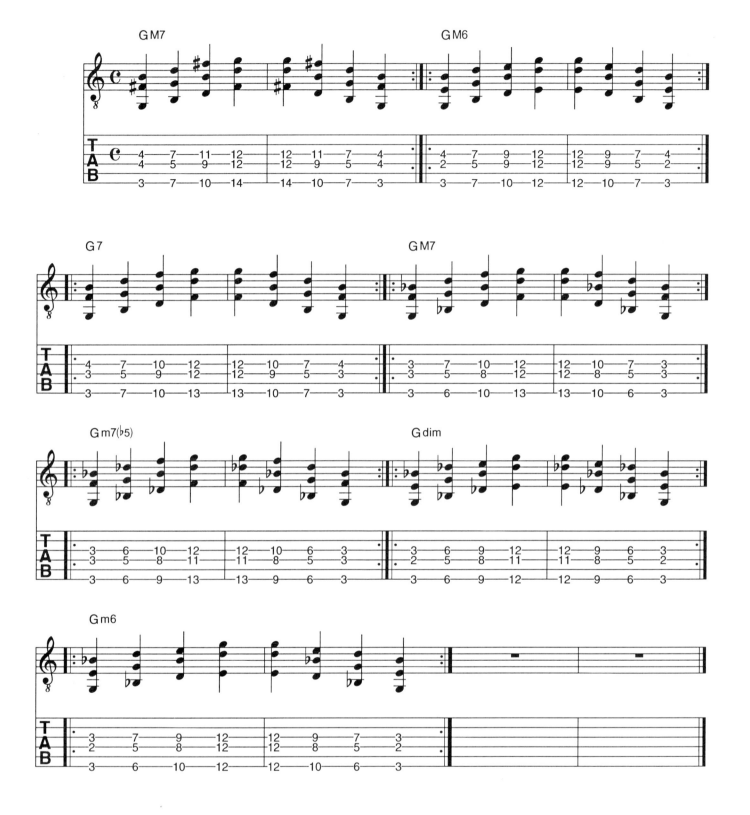

Let's back track a bit and talk about "4" to the bar. A rhythm guitarist in a band must be able to play "4" and "2" to the bar. This "2" to the bar is usually done on the 1st two choruses and the out chorus of a tune. The bassist plays on beats 1 and 3 while the guitarist plays on 2 and 4. Here's an example of playing on "2" to the bar and "4" to the bar on the tune "Out of Nowhere".

"COMPING" PART 3

In this lesson I'd like to talk about how one might approach using bass lines and chords for accompaniment. This is a rather difficult concept for many guitarists and to explain it on paper is also pretty tricky. The bass line idea is in a sense similar to the "4" to the bar we discussed in the earlier chapter and not unlike the tri-tone sub lesson. The one primary ingredient in negotiating this technique is to make sure that the bass notes are not picked in the same way you would normally pick. The way I use the pick here is to actually take a rhythm stroke as if you were playing all six strings but only hit the sixth string. This way it doesn't sound like it's actually plucked, therefore getting a more rhythmic sound. The technique for playing the 5th string I'll address in a bit. I rarely if ever play bass notes on the 4th string, as the sound is too thin. The thought to keep in mind as you play these bass notes is to be sure you play only that one string and mute or some how avoid the others. With the 6th string, that's not too difficult. The 5th string is another story. Let's begin a simple exercise using a Gm7th chord and see how you might approach this.

Example 1

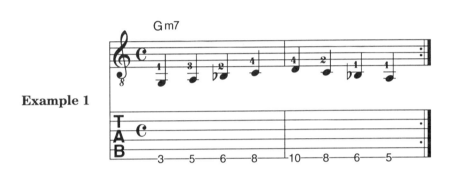

Play this exercise very staccato at first and keep the idea in mind that you're playing a rhythm guitar and get into a swinging groove. You might try using the side of the pick for a more percussive attack.

After getting the feel for this, you can start using a little "trick" that most bass players often use. It's a pull-off of one or more notes. Here's the music to show you what I mean.

Example 2

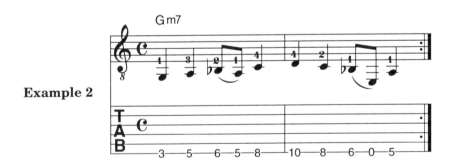

You can see that the A note in measure 1 and the E note in measure 2 are not picked but slurred (pull-off). Let's now talk about the 5th string bass line. This is not as easy as the 6th string as you'll have to find a way to mute the other strings while still using a full rhythmic pick hand. The reason for this full rhythm idea is if you pluck the notes instead of using a rhythmic approach, it sounds like a counter melody instead of accompaniment. The way I do it is mute the 6th string with my thumb (without strain of course). Here is the same exercise as example 2 using a Cm chord on the 5th string.

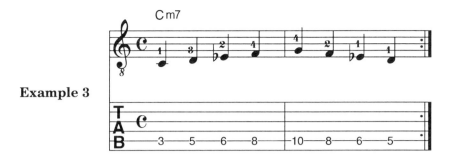

Example 3

Now with the pull-offs.

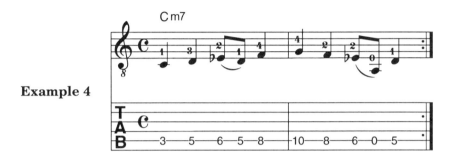

Example 4

While some of these notes may not be 100% harmonically accurate, it's of little difference as we're reaching more for a rhythmic attack. Listen to someone like Eddie Gomez for this idea of pull-offs and grooving with the rhythm.

When you are familiar with the bass line, adding chords here and there is a very effective comping tool. Here is example 1 with some added chords.

Example 5

The chords must be struck short (staccato) while maintaining that nice groove with the bass notes. Here's the same exercise using the pull-offs.

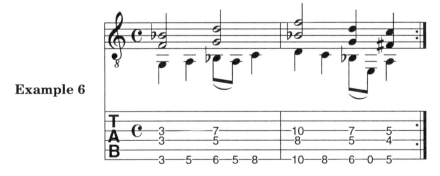

Example 6

The 5th string is again more difficult but can be done with some practice. Here is example 3 with some added chords.

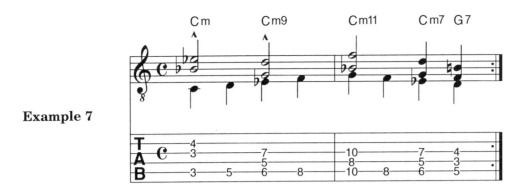

Example 7

Let's apply this technique to a II, V, I, VI pattern using approach bass notes (or tri-tone subs) in the key of G major.

Example 8

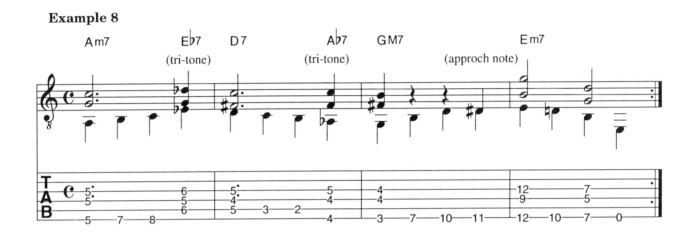

Here now is the A section of *Autumn Leaves* in the key or G.

Example 9

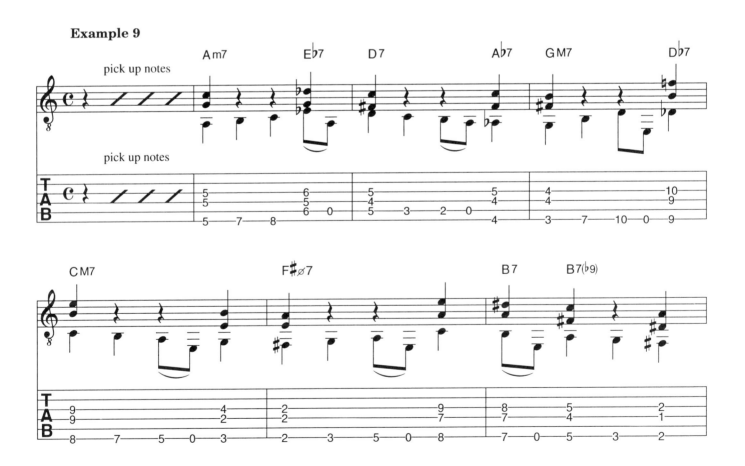

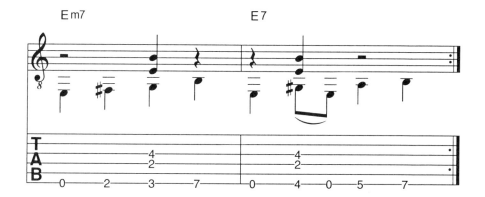

You'll notice that there are many inversions and passing chords. E.G. The E♭7 in bar 1 is a passing chord to D7. This technique is effective for any duo setting minus a bassist. Another effective way of using this technique is finger style. Without the pick, it's a bit easier as you play the bass note with the thumb and chords with the other fingers.

So far we've dealt with II-V-I-VI patterns with 4 beats per chord.

I'd like now to show the same patterns using 2 beats per chord. This is essentially the same as the tri-tone sub. Here are some examples in several keys.

Example 10

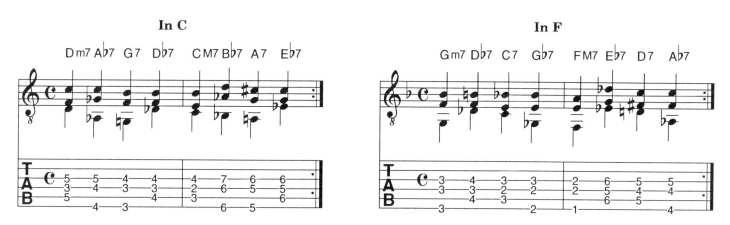

This can be a bit stiff keeping the same pattern so it's good to play it with some rhythmic variety. Here is an example of this same pattern with some added rhythm.

Example 11

Here's a blues progression in the key of G at a tempo of 108. The first bar is a pattern that's from ragtime piano (also the basis of "Blue Monk"). It's a very effective method of going from the I chord to the IV chord.

13

Example 12

This is a small overview of a very large picture. Comping is a wonderful art form and can be learned with listening and application of basic rules. It's also great fun to swing hard and listen to the soloists have such a good time with your great accompaniment! Enjoy!

JACK WILKINS JAZZ TIPS:

Using your left-hand thumb for chording

When I was a beginning student, I had never seen a guitarist use their thumb for chords so it hadn't occurred to me to do this. After listening to Tal Farlow and Barney Kessel recordings, and trying to play what I could from them, I found it impossible to play certain chords.

A friend of mine helped my education by showing me how Tal and Barney had accomplished this seemingly impossible feat by simply using the thumb. Some years later I had the good fortune to see Tal and Barney play live and saw it with my own eyes! They indeed used their thumb often and who can argue with their results? Now I use it all the time. It seems to me that you can get much wider and sustained chords as well as being able to play these voicings much more easily.

In the first two examples we'll use a II-V-I pattern in the key of G and D.

Example 1

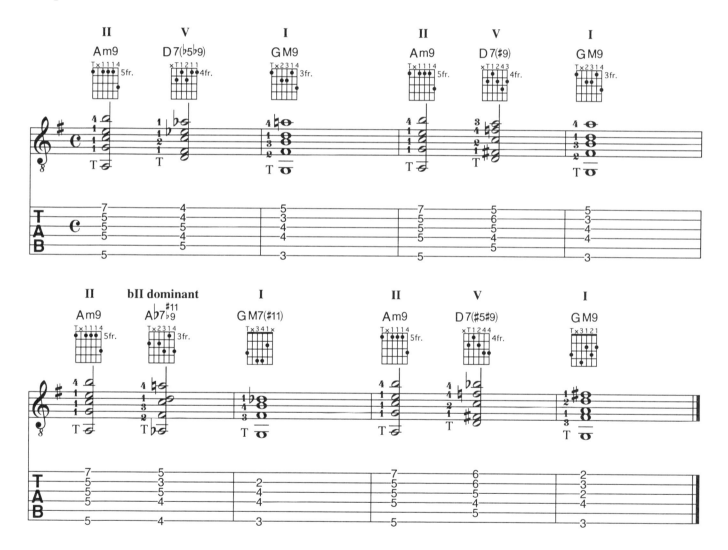

Example 2

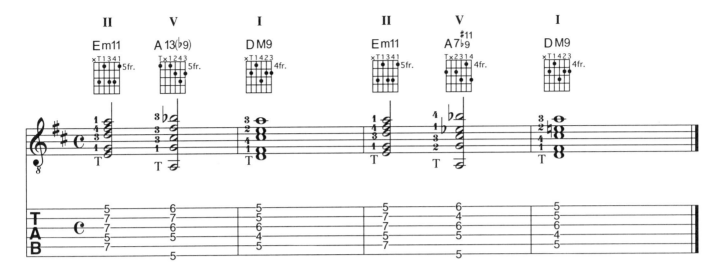

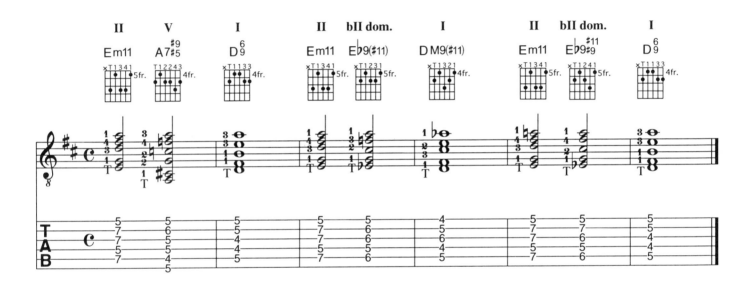

Example 3 shows triads on top of a pedal bass using the thumb.

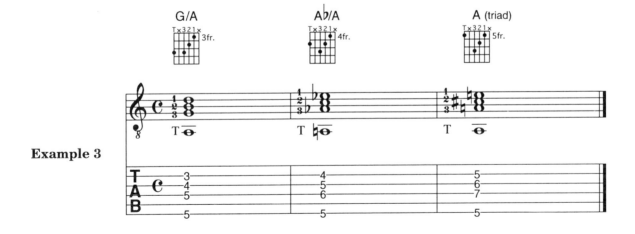

Example 3

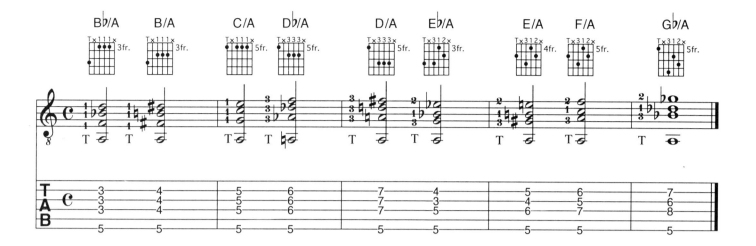

In translating the II-V-I pattern to minor, the V chord (or bII) is the same as in the major key. However, the II and I chords would be different. Instead of minor 7ths, the II chord would be a 1/2 diminished 7th. The I chord, of course, would be minor. Example 4 shows these voicings.

Example 4

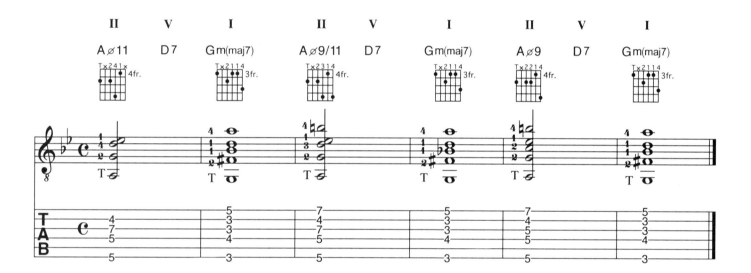

Example 5 is a cycle of 5ths often used by Joe Pass among others. I find using the thumb here to be far smoother and easier mainly because the 1st and 3rd finger never alter.

Example 5

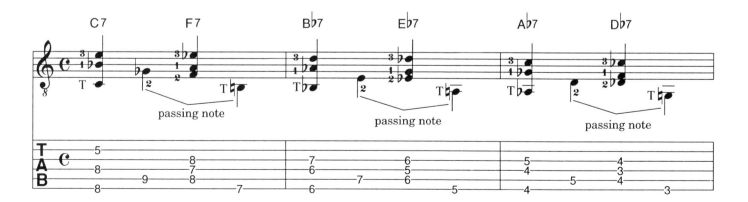

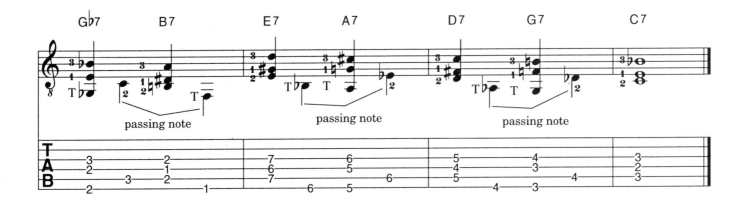

On those passing notes you could play the chord instead of the note but it could sound a bit overdone. In trying to use the thumb in this way it might be contorted at first. The key is to simply *relax the left hand* and by practice find a way to "turn" the hand slightly to achieve it. I think it's worth some experimentation since we all want to get the most out of the guitar as possible. Till next time.

Jack Wilkins Jazz Tips:

Inner voices

Have you ever wondered how players like George Van Eps, Johnny Smith, Chuck Wayne, Ted Greene, Gene Bertincini, Howard Alden, etc., often times sound like two guitarists at once? One "trick" is to sustain the melody and bass (outer voices), while moving the inner voices. This may sound a bit complicated but a few exercises will show you how to incorporate this technique into your playing. For starters, if you play a simple CM7 chord with the 5th string root (example A) then omit the G on the 4th string and change the fingering (example B).

Example A   **Example B**

You're now in position for moving inner voices. You must hold down (sustain) your second and fourth finger (bass and melody) while changing the third finger (3rd string) on the 4th fret to the first finger on the 2nd fret (3rd string).

This can be done with either the pick, fingers, or you can slur the note provided you mute the strings you aren't playing. The outer voices must sustain while changing the inner voices. This is a gentle move!

Technically, you're playing a CM7 to a CM6, but I prefer to think of this as a moving inner voice. If we were to play a diatonic pattern in C major, it would look like this:

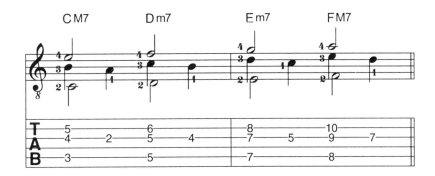

Different inner voices can be used as in the following examples:

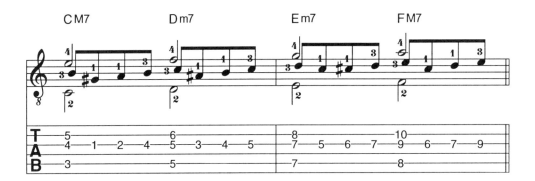

The same principle applies if we used the 6th string root.

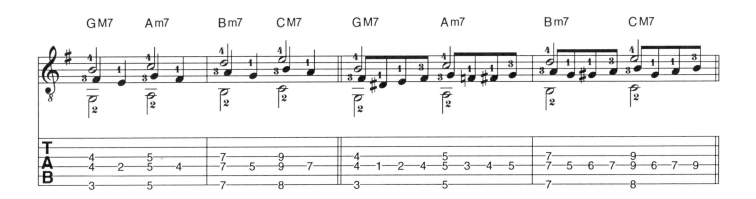

This inner voice technique is useful for playing solo guitar or perhaps while accompanying a singer. In addition, it can be used for intros or endings. Here are a few examples using moving inner voices:

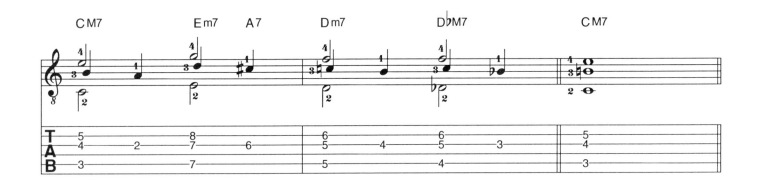

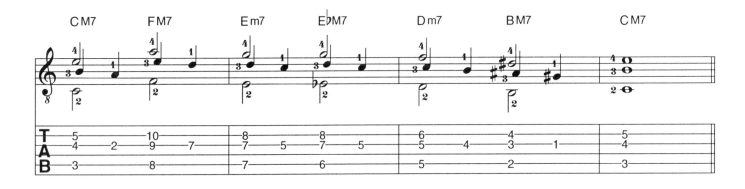

20

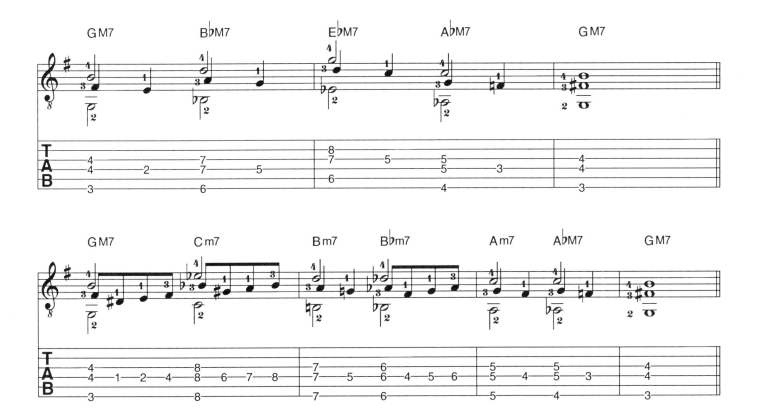

If you're interested in further study, I recommend Van Eps' classic book, "Harmonic Mechanisms for Guitar." Until next time.

Jack Wilkins Jazz Tips:

Intros Part 1

I thought it might be fun to write introductions to a few standard tunes in this issue and the next. I've chosen a variety of songs, some starting on the tonic, some on the II chord, one starting on the IV as well as different tempos, major and minor keys.

I've used various techniques, primarily contrary motion. (For example, bass note goes down, top note goes up.) Most of the intros are four bars in length while number 4 is eight bars. Of course, you could play the 4 bar intros twice!

These intros might be used for many different songs (as long as the beginning of the song starts on the same chord change!). See how many songs you could think of using these intros.

I'll return next issue and tell you what songs I had in mind! Have fun!

Example 1

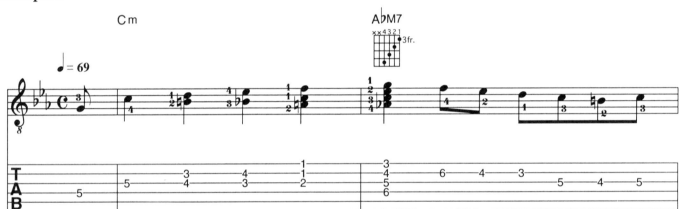

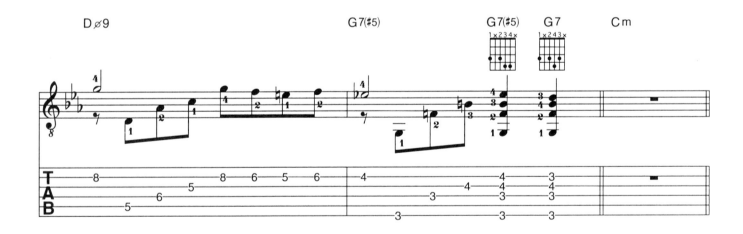

Example 2

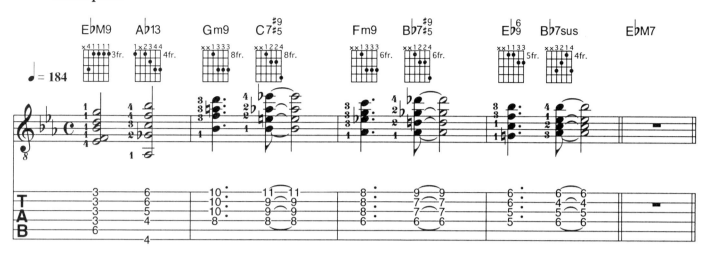

Example 3

Example 4

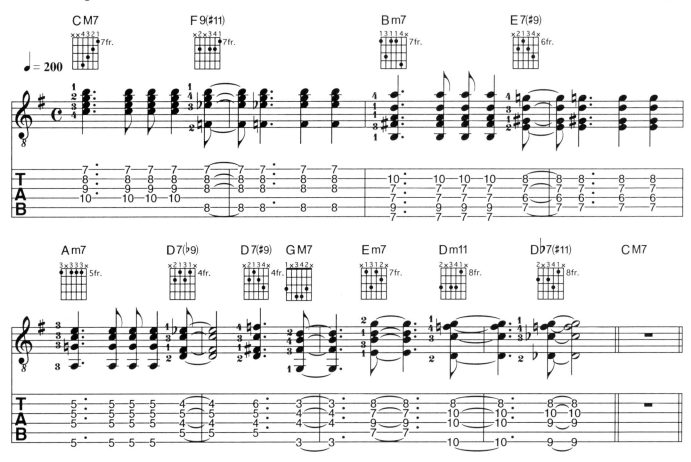

Example 5

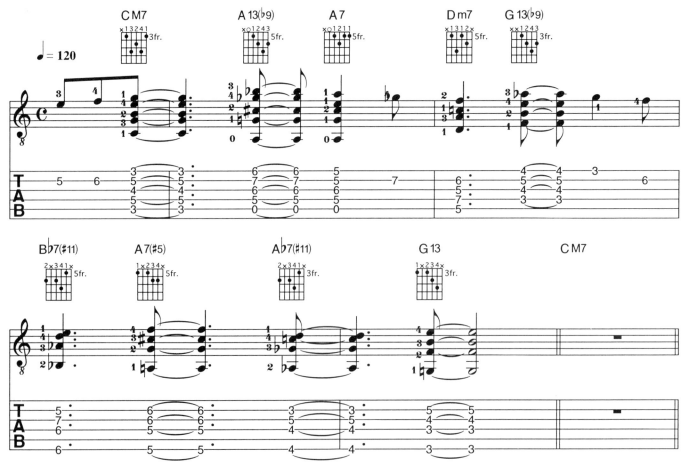

24

JACK WILKINS JAZZ TIPS:

Intros Part 2

As a follow up to the May 1998 issue. I've included five more intros for you to play (the same text applies for these intros).

While playing the previous intros. I'm sure you found they could work for a number of different songs. However, the songs I had in mind from the May issue are as follows:

1. My Funny Valentine
2. It Could Happen to You
3. Body and Soul
4. Just Friends
5. My Romance

I hope you enjoy these new intros and I'll return next time and tell you what songs I had in mind. Jack!

Example 6

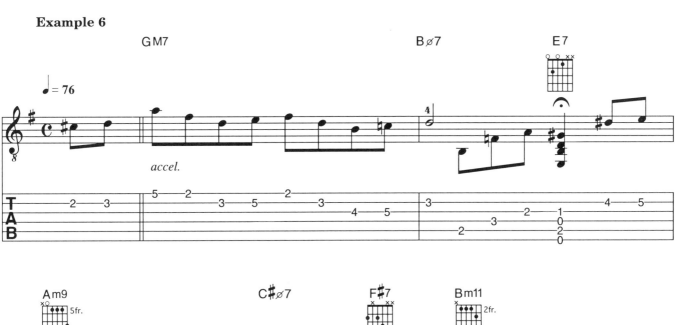

Example 7

Example 8

Example 9

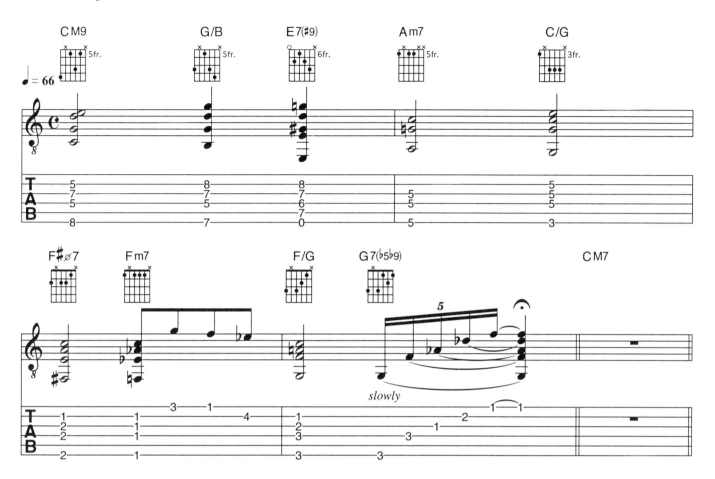

Example 10

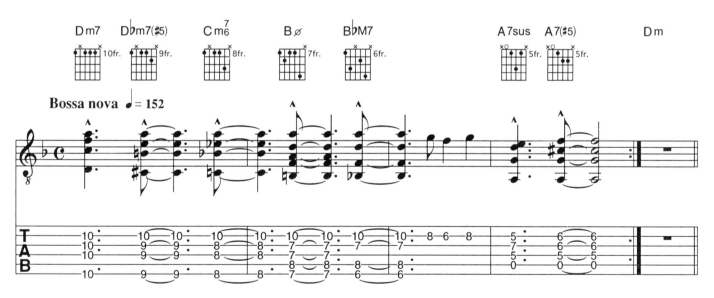

Jack Wilkins Jazz Tips:

Endings Part 1

The logical extension of the May '98 and August '98 issues of intros is now to try ten endings. I've decided to use the same tunes we used for intros. (I'm sure you'll hear what the tunes are now.)

All of these songs end on the tonic chord. (For example, GM in the key of G.) The bar or bars before the endings are the II chord (Am7 in G) to the V chord (D7 in G). I intentionally made the rhythms as easy as possible so when you play these endings you could make them as interesting rhythmically as you wish.

Example 1 is a common enough ending that you've heard before. The "chords" are just parallel fourths.

Example 2 is contrary motion. For example, bass and mid-tone move down and upper voice goes up and down. These are not really "chords" but simple voicings (except for the last CM7).

Example 3 is another conventional ending that is good to have in your repertoire.

Examples 4 and 5 are also conventional but helpful to have on hand!

Getting back to the August issue, the five remaining tunes I had in mind were;
1. But Beautiful
2. Emily
3. Gone with the Wind
4. My One and Only Love
5. How Insensitive

Hope you enjoy… Next issue I'll have the remaining five endings.

Example 1

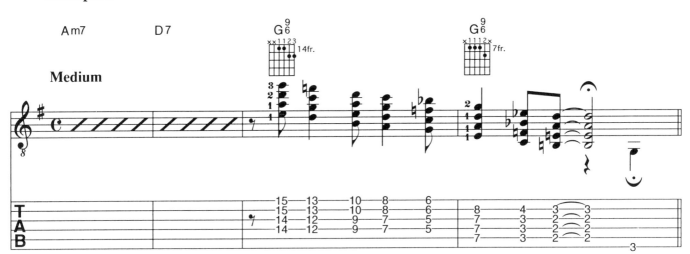

28

Example 2

Ballad

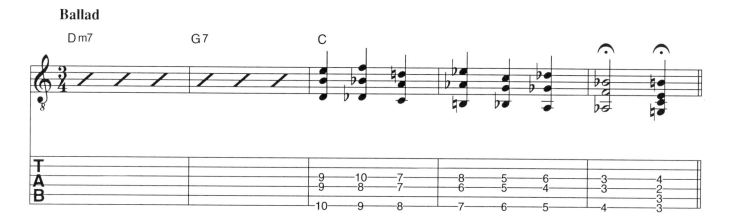

Example 3

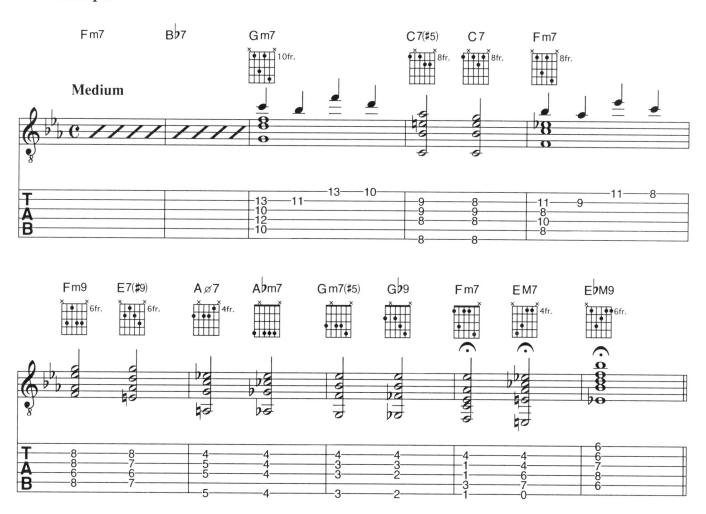

29

Example 4

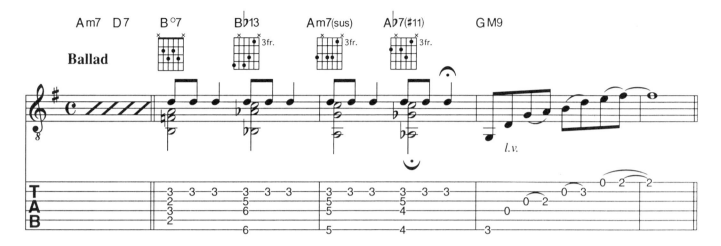

Example 5

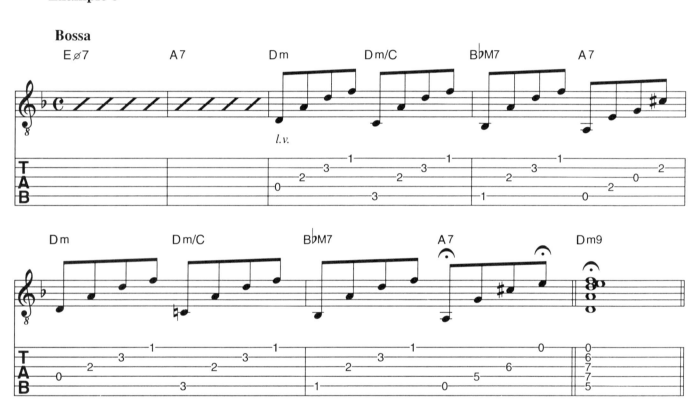

JACK WILKINS JAZZ TIPS:
Endings Part 2

The follow-up of the November issue of endings are the remaining 5 songs. (By now you probably know what song I had in mind.) Looking at example 1 of this issue, a very common idea for ending a tune is to go to a different key with the tonic note on top. In this case C is the tonic with an AbM7 underneath. Example 2 is essentially the same idea with the C♯ (or Db) on top and an AM7 underneath. In both examples the chord before the last chord is a sharp I or (flat II). For example:

1. Db to C
2. D to Db

Example 3 is a very conventional progression of II V (Fmi7 Bb7) to III VI (Gm7 C7) back to II V to a "Count" Basie ending. (You can't have ten endings without at least one Count Basie!)

Example 4 ends in Eb major but the tune is actually in C minor. Try to sustain the chords throughout.

Looking at example 5 you'll notice that in bar 3, I've written Em9, A7 ♯5 ♯9, Dm9 and G7 ♯5 ♯9. All these chords are minus the root. If you can add the root, all the better.

Hope you enjoy these endings!

Here are the tunes I had in mind for the November issue:

1. Just Friends
2. Emily
3. Gone with the Wind
4. But Beautiful
5. How Insensitive

Example 1 - C major

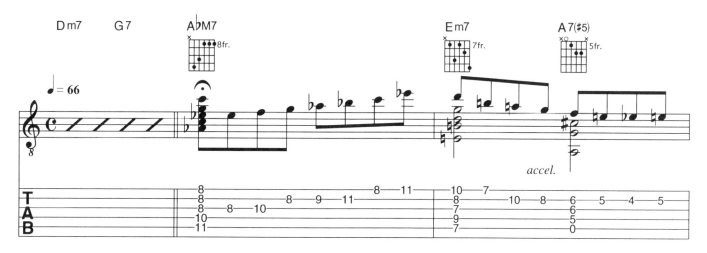

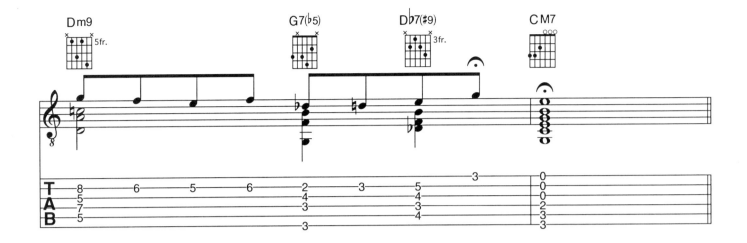

Example 2 - D♭ major

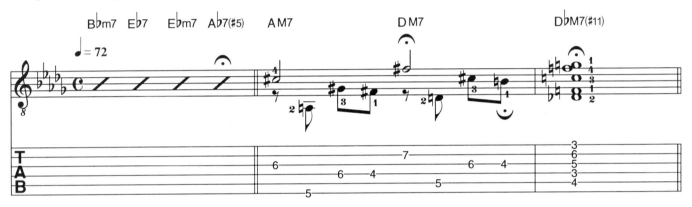

Example 3 - E♭ major

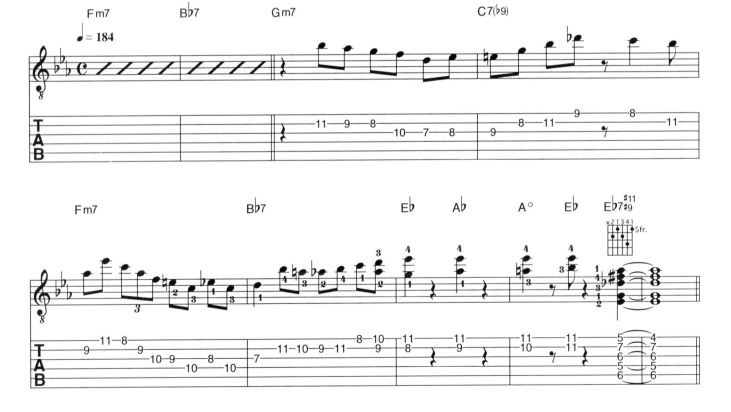

Example 4 - C minor

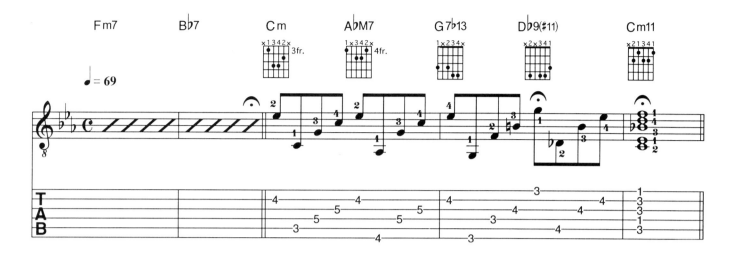

Example 5 - C major

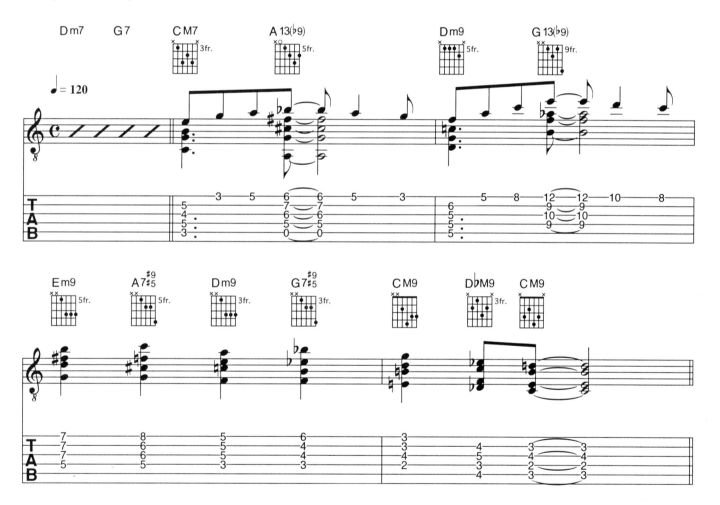

The five last tunes for endings are:

Ex. 1: My One + Only Love

Ex. 2: Body + Soul

Ex. 3: Gone with the Wind

Ex. 4: My Funny Valentine

Ex. 5: My Romance

JACK WILKINS JAZZ TIPS:

Tri-tone substitution

The tri-tone substitution is a very common device in jazz music. Although used often, it isn't readily understood. What is a tri-tone? The Harvard dictionary of music defines it as "the interval of the diminished fifth, C to Gb, or augmented fourth, C to F♯, so called because it spans three whole tones."

This definition doesn't mean much to a student trying to cope with tri-tone substitutions!

The first thing a student must learn are all the tri-tone or diminished fifth intervals in all the keys. Example: C to Gb, D to Ab, G to Db, etc. A simplified way of explaining how one would use the tri-tone substitution is this:

Take a C7 chord and substitute a Gb7 chord for it (C to Gb tri-tone). The tri-tone works mainly with the dominant chords. Example: take a II-V-I-VI$_x$ (x meaning dominant) progression in the key of F.

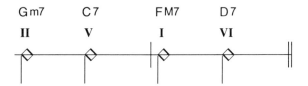

Using the tri-tone system, you could "substitute" the following chords using the same II-V-I-VI$_x$ progression.
Example:

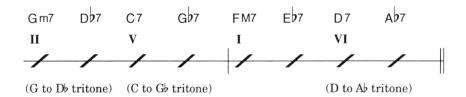

(The Eb7 to D7 is a chromatic approach.)

You'll see how the "substitute" chords are a colorful way of playing simple progressions.

Here are some voicings using the standard II-V-I-VI$_x$ progressions.

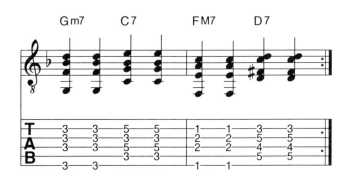

And now with the tri-tone substitutions.

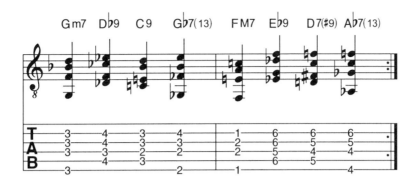

You'll see I've altered the quality of some of the chords in this progression. Example: D♭9 for D♭7 or G♭13 for G♭7, etc. The important lesson here is to understand how the tri-tone works. Notice how the bass line operates.

G D♭ C G♭ F E♭ D A♭

Some players refer to this pattern as a chromatic approach. That's fine! Whatever you wish to call it, it's a great sound. (Listen to *Art Tatum* or Joe Pass for some incredible use of this concept.)

As a practice, here are the changes to *Autumn Leaves* in standard progression.

Here is the same pattern with tri-tones.

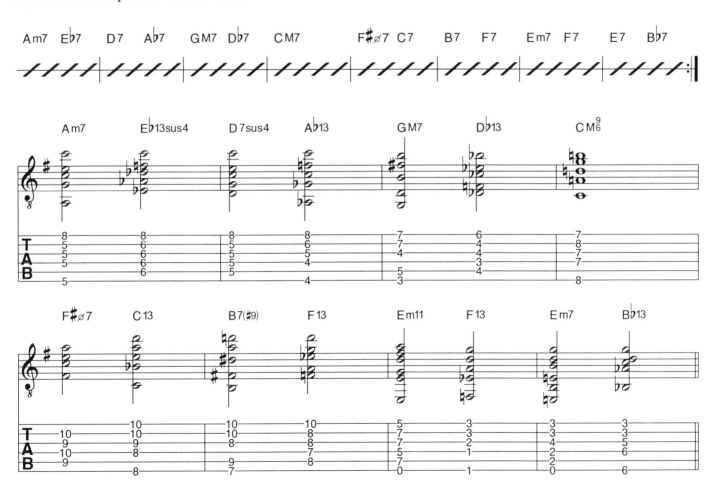

35

Here again I've altered the quality of the chords for a fuller and more expansive sound. Example: E♭13sus4 for E♭7, etc. I've also tried to make effective use of contrary motion. Example: the D♭ 13 to Cmaj$^9_6$. The top note B♭ goes up to B♮ while the bottom. D♭ goes down to C. Here are the conventional "changes" to "Rhythm" (I Got Rhythm).

I GOT RHYTHM

"A" Section

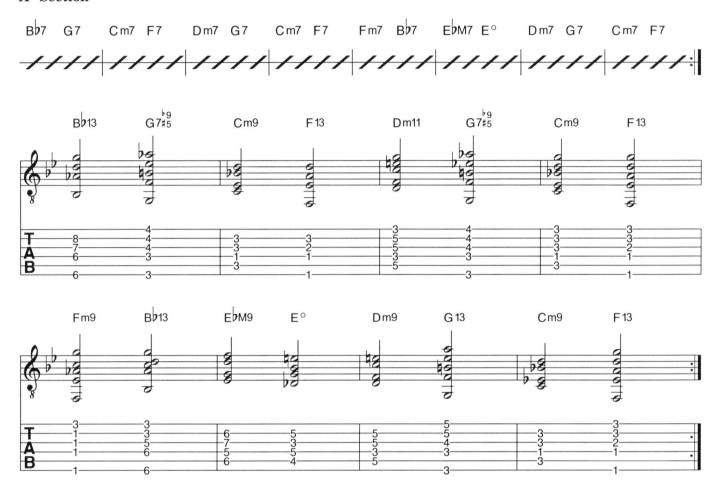

Now with tri-tones:

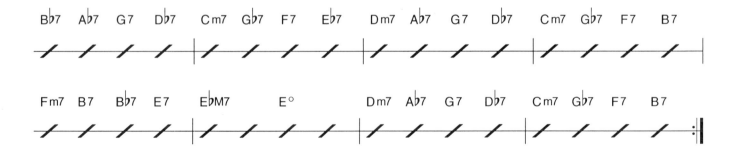

36

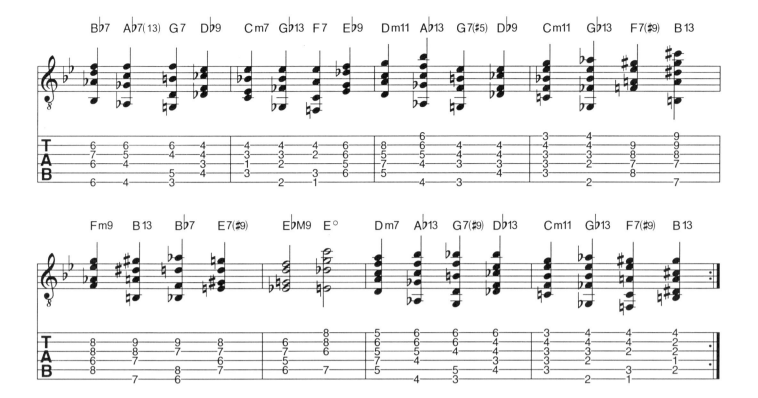

This is very full! One probably wouldn't use all these changes, but as practice, it couldn't hurt. So, as usual, practice, experiment and listen!

Till next time.

Jack Wilkins Jazz Tips:
6 Basic Fingerings

Most guitarists on the intermediate level know practically every scale and arpeggio by now, but one of the problems I've encountered with my students is they rarely play these scales and arpeggios in any organized manner.

I've found that the simplest way to learn these scales and arpeggios is to use the "6 Basic Fingerings." These fingerings lay very nicely on the fretboard and cover the whole range of the guitar. This time we'll just work on major and minor scales and major 7th arpeggios.

The "6 Basic Fingerings" are:
> **6th String Root**: 1st, 2nd & 4th finger
> **5th String Root**: 1st, 2nd & 4th finger.

I'll use the A major and A minor scale and arpeggio from the 6th string root and the D major and D minor scale and arpeggio from the 5th string root.

Any scale or mode can be played using these "6." The 7th arpeggios include major 7, dominant 7, minor 7, half diminished 7, diminished 7, dominant 7#5, dominant 7b5. major 7#5, major 7b5, major 6, minor 6 and minor major 7. If you check out the "6 Basic Fingerings" you'll find each one of these arpeggios lay very nicely on the guitar.

Later on we'll work out all the 9th, 11th and 13th arpeggios.

Major Scales
A major

1st finger

2nd finger

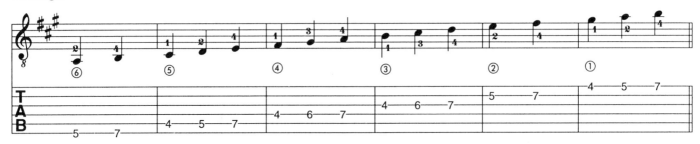

4th finger

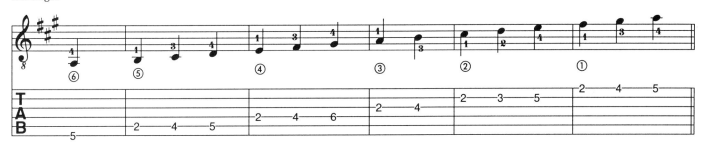

D major

1st finger

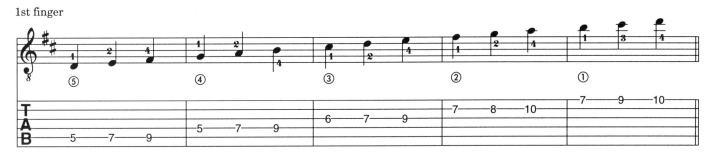

2nd finger

4th finger

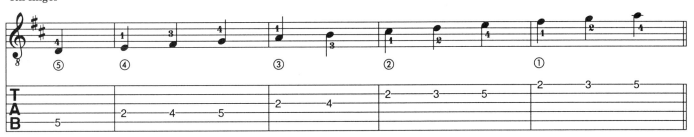

MELODIC MINOR SCALES
A minor

1st finger

2nd finger

4th finger

D minor

1st finger

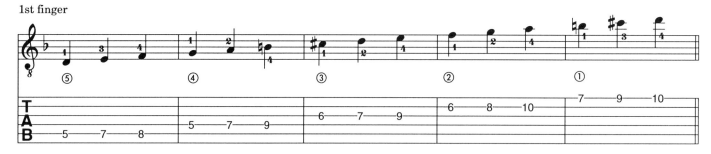

2nd finger

MAJOR 7TH ARPEGGIOS
A major 7th

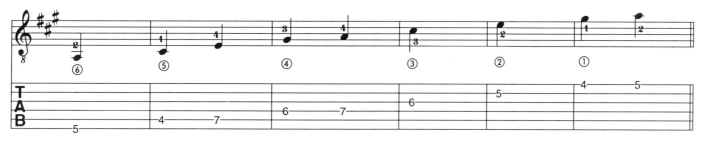

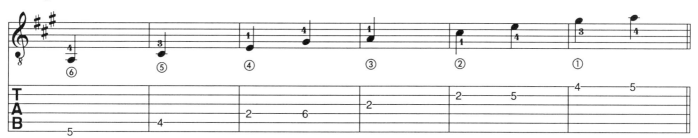

D major 7th

1st finger

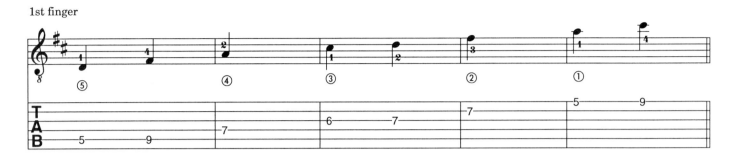

2nd finger

4th finger

42

JACK WILKINS JAZZ TIPS:
Altered scales

"Altered" scales! Much confusion exists about this. Words like "Lydian ♯5 Phrygian, Lydian ♯9" etc. scare everyone. The way I look at this is to simplify as much as possible. It's difficult enough improvising with good time and expression without having all these names to think about. Essentially I feel the player has to have the sound of the "altered" scale in their ear. For example, if I have an A7 chord to improvise on, I might think of A7♭9 or A7♯9. What scale would you play on A7♭9 or A7♯9? I think of this as B♭°!

Here is the A7♭9 or A7♯9 scale I might use.

Example 1

Analyze these notes.

Example 2

Taking the scale from B♭ you find you have a simple B♭ diminished scale (starting on A of course). The fingering for this scale would be:

Example 3

You could try the six basic fingerings for this "altered" scale. Some other altered scales could be as follows:

Example 4

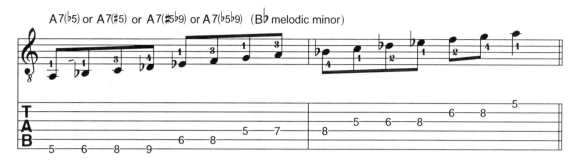

Analyzing this scale, it's nothing more than a B♭ melodic minor! (starting on A) or you might try a B♭ harmonic minor for A7♯5. For example:

Example 5

One possible "altered" scale for AM7♯5 could be F♯ melodic minor or F♯ harmonic minor.
For example:

Example 6

Example 7

The important aspect of all this is to analyze all of the possible alterations and then let the sounds become part of your basic musicianship. Listening to other players use these sound helped me to use them in my own playing. I do feel that simplifying would be far more productive! Till next time!!

Jack Wilkins Jazz Tips:
Picking

As a young student of the guitar, I had no real formula for how to use the guitar pick until I found Johnny Smith's book called "Aids to Technique". Since I was such a fan of his music, I wanted to learn how he played the way he did. I found he suggested alternate picking for everything. For several years I played with only this sort of articulation. Alternate picking is quite easy to understand, simply down stroke (⊓), then up stroke (V) throughout. (Pat Martino uses alternate, among many others.)

Later on I heard the magnificent guitarist Chuck Wayne, and saw he was as fast and smooth as Johnny but using a different picking technique altogether. Chuck called this picking "consecutive".

Barney Kesssel also used this picking and three guitarists today who use this technique are Frank Gambale, Carl Barry and Jimmy Bruno.

To understand "consecutive" or "sweep" picking, as some guitarists call it; when crossing strings going "down" the guitar, play a down stroke ("down" the guitar meaning, for example, going from the A string to the D string, or G string to the B string). Then play an up stroke crossing strings while going "up" the guitar. ("up" the guitar meaning, for example, going from the B string to the G string).

Here is a scale exercise using consecutive picking.

Down stroke = ⊓   Up stroke = V

Example 1

G major scale

The fingering on this G major scale works very well for consecutive picking.

When crossing strings using down strokes, the pick hand has a tendency to rest the pick on the following string. This is fine, but on the up stroke the pick hand has a tendency to pick away, or turn away from the string. Be careful of too much movement of the pick hand.

When practicing any scale or arpeggio, try to keep a nice $\frac{4}{4}$ tempo. Here are some exercises using consecutive picking.

Example 2

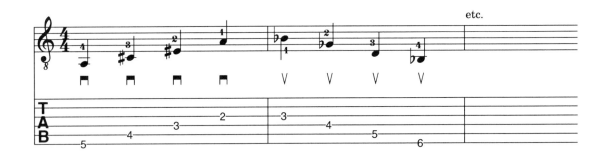

You'll notice the next four exercises start with an up stroke.

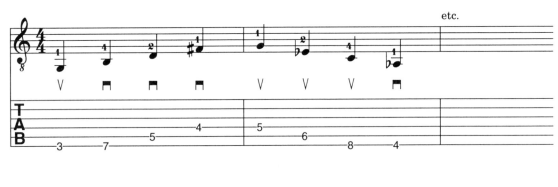

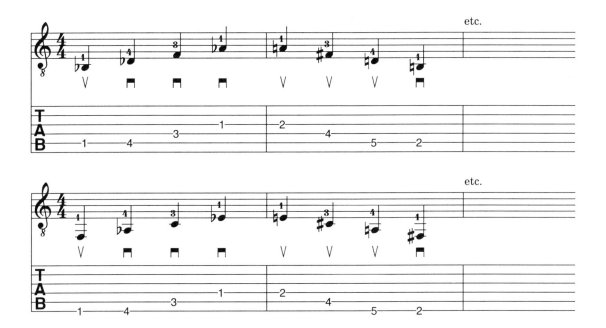

After looking at some of the possibilities of consecutive picking, you'll see how it can be an effective way of playing certain phrases.

Another way of picking articulation is slur picking, which means not picking each and every note. This can be a very smooth and effective way of playing up tempos.

Allan Holdsmith uses mostly slurs in his playing and Jimmy Raney used slur picking quite a bit.

The trick to slur picking is to make sure the note you are slurring to is "hammered" with a strong left hand.

Here are some scales using slur picking.

Slurs are marked with ⌒ .

Example 3

47

As you see, the slurs can be optional. You'll have to experiment to find the best way for you. Here is a GM7 arpeggio combining slurs and consecutive picking.

Example 4

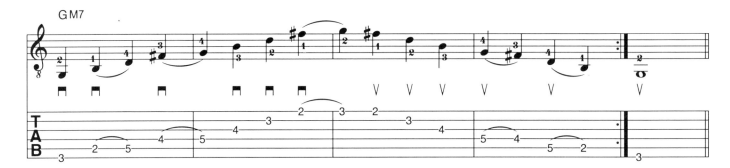

You might try these different picking techniques using the six basic fingerings (scales and arpeggios), as demonstrated in the August 1996 issue.

Here is a G diminished scale using the three different picking techniques.

Example 5

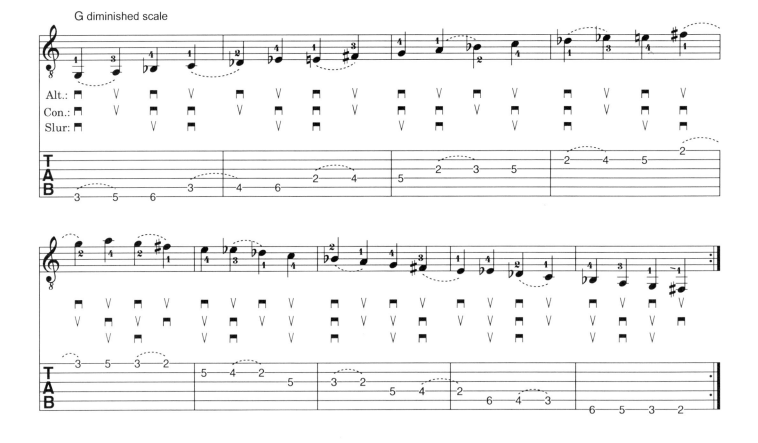

Lastly, here are some alternate picking exercises which I have found to be very helpful.

Example 6

You might try going up and down the guitar chromatically.

Example 7

Example 8

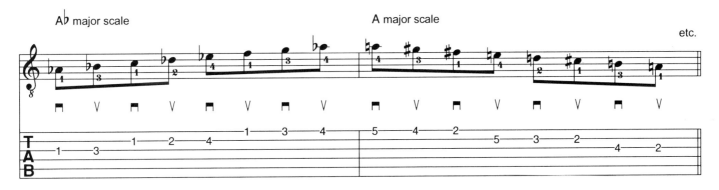

Example 9

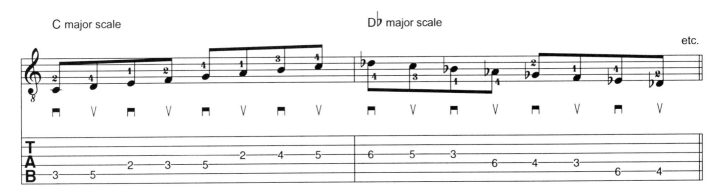

Example 10

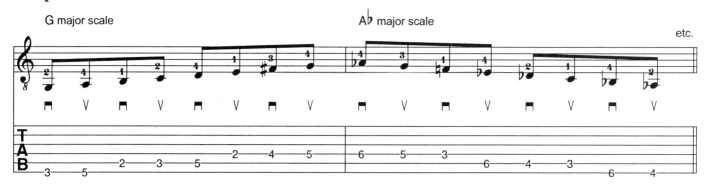

Example 11

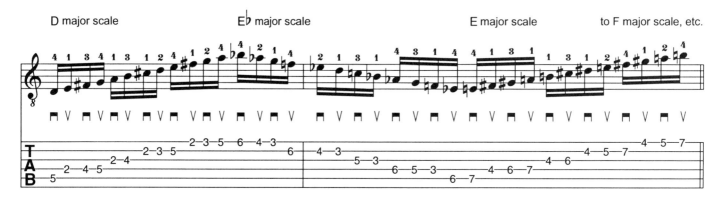

All these exercises should be practiced very slowly at first. The speed will come with relaxation and control.

In my own playing, I use a combination of all three techniques. I think the phrase you are playing dictates which sort of picking to be used. As usual, experimentation and practice will help you decide what works best for you.

Jack Wilkins Jazz Tips:

Arpeggio extensions

In the August issue of JJG, we talked about the "6 Basic Fingerings." They are 6th string root: 1st, 2nd, and 4th fingers: 5th string root: 1st, 2nd, and 4th fingers. Applying these fingerings to any scale, mode or arpeggio is very logical and fits beautifully on the guitar.

This issue we'll deal with some of the arpeggio extensions using the keys of A major (6th string root) and D major (5th string root). We'll work on six common arpeggio extensions (extensions meaning 9th, 11th and 13th).

The arpeggio extensions we'll use are:

major $\sharp11\atop13$, 9 $\sharp11\atop13$, 7$\flat$9$\sharp11\atop13$, 7$\sharp$9$\sharp11\atop13$, minor 9$11\atop13$ and half diminished 9$\sharp11\atop13$.

Of course, there are other arpeggio extensions but in the interest of space, these six are enough. Looking these over, you'll notice that some of the 5th string root arpeggios don't lay well for a complete two octaves. In those cases I've added a 1st finger slide. In practicing, be sure to start slowly and keep a definite rhythm going up and down. (A metronome is a very helpful tool.)

Key of A Major Arpeggio Extensions

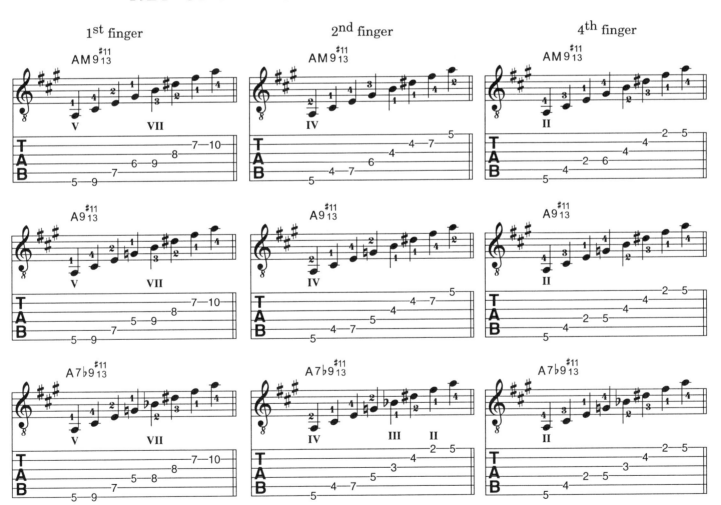

51

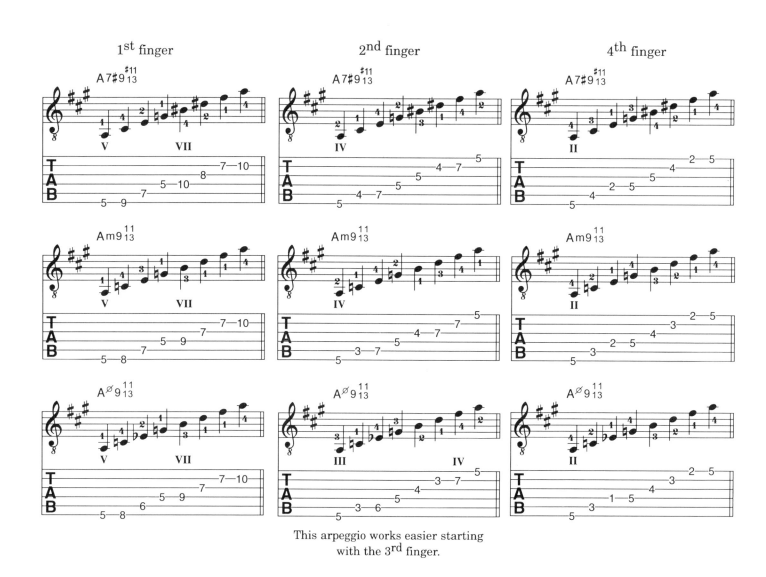

This arpeggio works easier starting
with the 3rd finger.

KEY OF D MAJOR ARPEGGIO EXTENSIONS

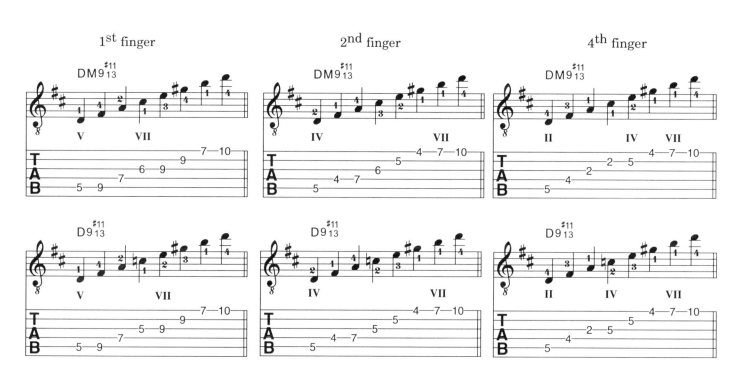

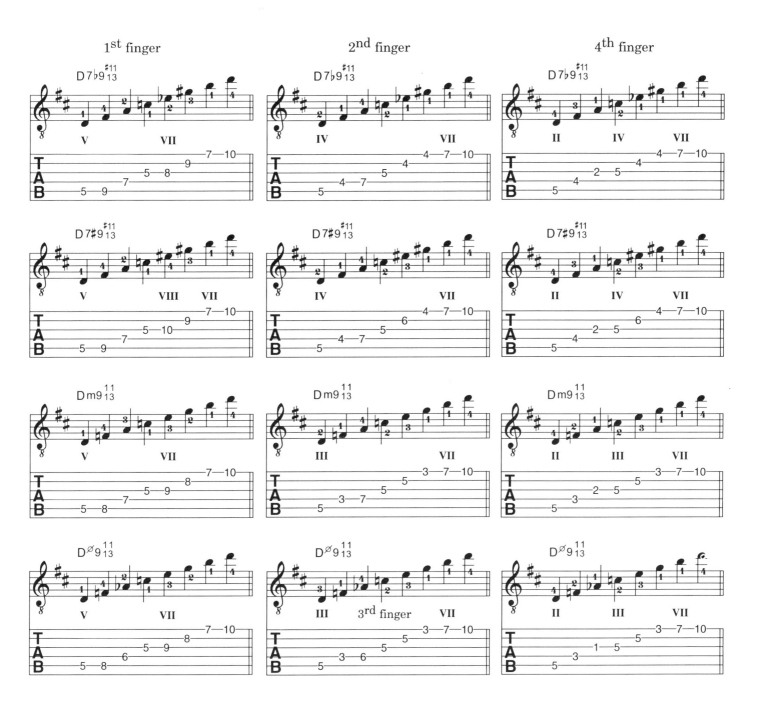

Notice that these arpeggio extensions actually combine two separate 7th arpeggios. For example:

AM9 $^{\sharp11}_{13}$ is AM7 (A, C♯, E, G♯) and B7 (B, D♯, F♯, A).

In further study you'll find a combination of 7 triads:

AM9 $^{\sharp11}_{13}$ is AM, C♯m, EM, G♯m, BM, D♯°, F♯m.

There are seven 7th chords:

AM9 $^{\sharp11}_{13}$ is AM7, C♯m7, EM7, G♯m7, B7, D♯7°, F♯m7.

As you look over the other arpeggios, you'll find different triads and 7th chords. In studying all this, always remember that these are just suggested fingerings, not always to be taken literally. Each person has their own way of playing and the ideal is to find the best way for you.

Be creative and open to new ideas in your study!

Jack Wilkins Jazz Tips:

Approach notes

In this lesson I'd like to discuss approach notes! Simply stated, approach notes are the notes above or below the targeted note.

For example, if you play a C triad arpeggio and play the approach note below it would look like this:

Example 1

fingerings: (1 - 2)   (1 - 1)   (3 - 4)   (3 - 4)   (2 - 3)   (1 - 2)   (1 - 2)

(Approach notes are the dark notes.) These notes don't necessarily have to be half steps below, they can be whole steps as well.

Example 2

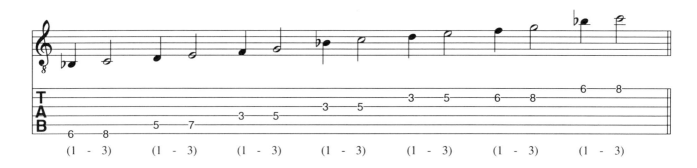

(1 - 3)   (1 - 3)   (1 - 3)   (1 - 3)   (1 - 3)   (1 - 3)   (1 - 3)

Here's where you can experiment with playing half step or whole step approach notes.

Example 3

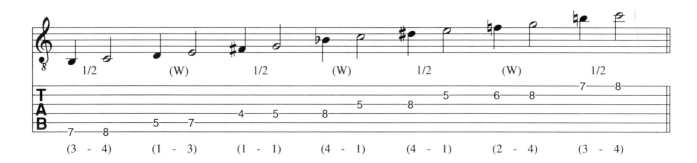

(3 - 4)   (1 - 3)   (1 - 1)   (4 - 1)   (4 - 1)   (2 - 4)   (3 - 4)

Now let's try the approach note above the targeted note using half steps.

Example 4

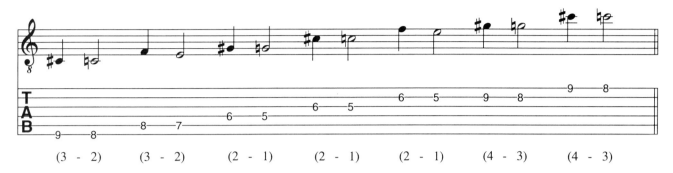

Next try it using whole steps.

Example 5

Finally, a combination of whole and half steps.

Example 6

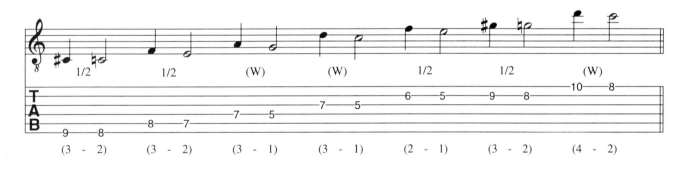

You'll hear how a simple C major triad arpeggio can be extremely colorful! Now let's combine above and below approach notes and play the same C triad arpeggio.

Example 7

Here again you can vary the approach note any way you wish. For example, start with an above note, then below to the target note.

Example 8

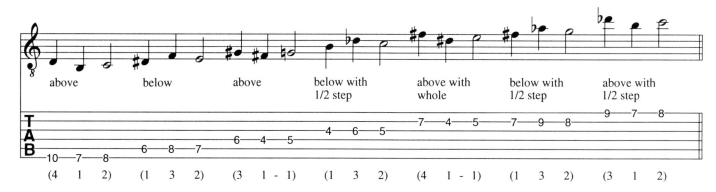

So far, we've dealt with one or two approach notes. Let's now try using three approach notes (still using C triad arpeggio). This exercise, I've put in a tempo. This will be two above - one below!

Example 9

Now try two below, one above.

Example 10

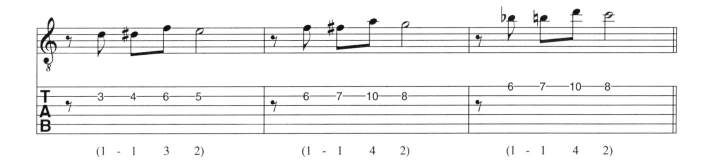

Now combine music examples 9 and 10. (The targeted notes fall on beats one and three.) Pay close attention to the fingerings.

Example 11

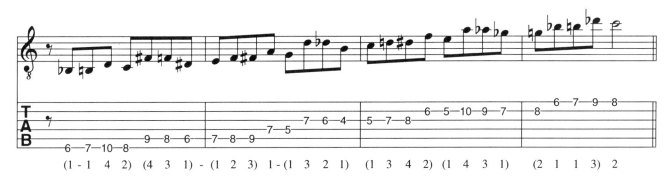

Finally, let's try a four note pattern still using C triad: below / above / above / below.

Example 12

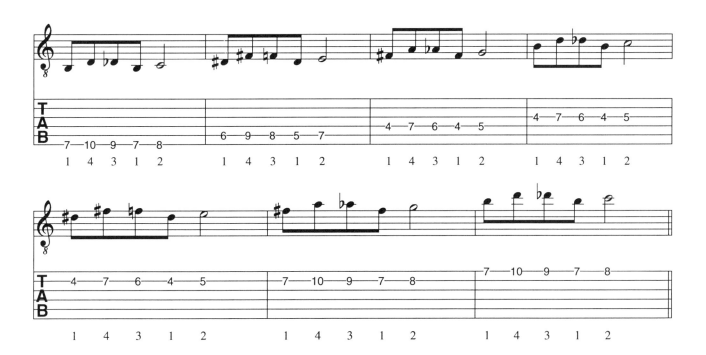

As you can see the possibilities are endless. You can use above, below, half or whole steps or 1, 2, 3 or 4 approach notes. You can also try exercises using any arpeggio you want. Here is a Gm9 arpeggio using the principles from the twelve exercises.

Example 13

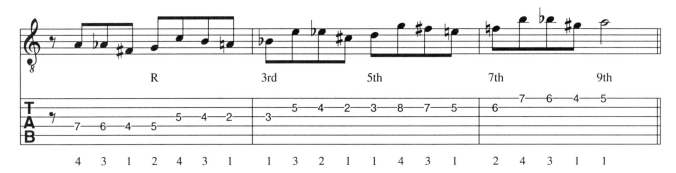

R   3rd   5th   7th   9th

```
                                    5—4—2—3—8—7—5      7—6—4—5
                      5—4—2   3                  6
              7—6—4—5
```

4   3   1   2   4   3   1   1   3   2   1   1   4   3   1   2   4   3   1   1

So, experiment, practice and explore the possibilities of approach notes.
Til next time.

Intro to Four Solos (Jack Wilkins)

The following four solos are not part of "Just Jazz Guitar" lessons. I have included these as a way of introducing some interesting and informative fingerings that I feel are helpful in the execution of difficult phrases on the guitar. At first you may find these fingerings a bit odd but if you keep working them out, I think you'll see how much easier these phrases will flow. The picking of these solos I've left up to the student as I've found over the years each player seem to have their own way of using the pick. Some use alternate, some consecutive (or "sweep" picking), and some use slur picking. You might try different ways of picking after you learn the solos. Consult the chapter on "Picking Techniques" for more information. Have fun!

MELS BLUES

Jack Wilkins

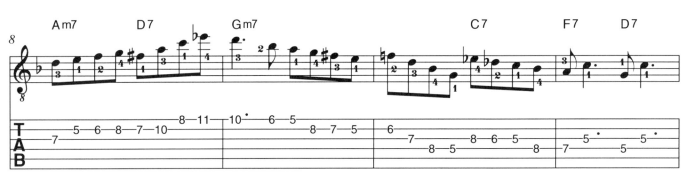

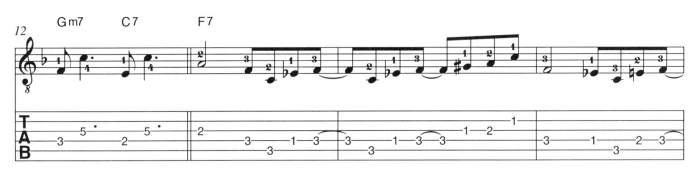

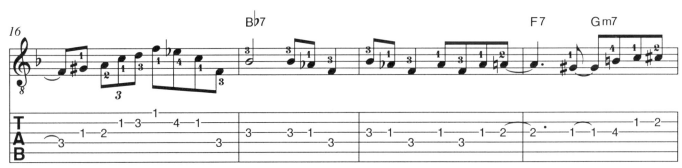

Speak Low for Me

Jack Wilkins

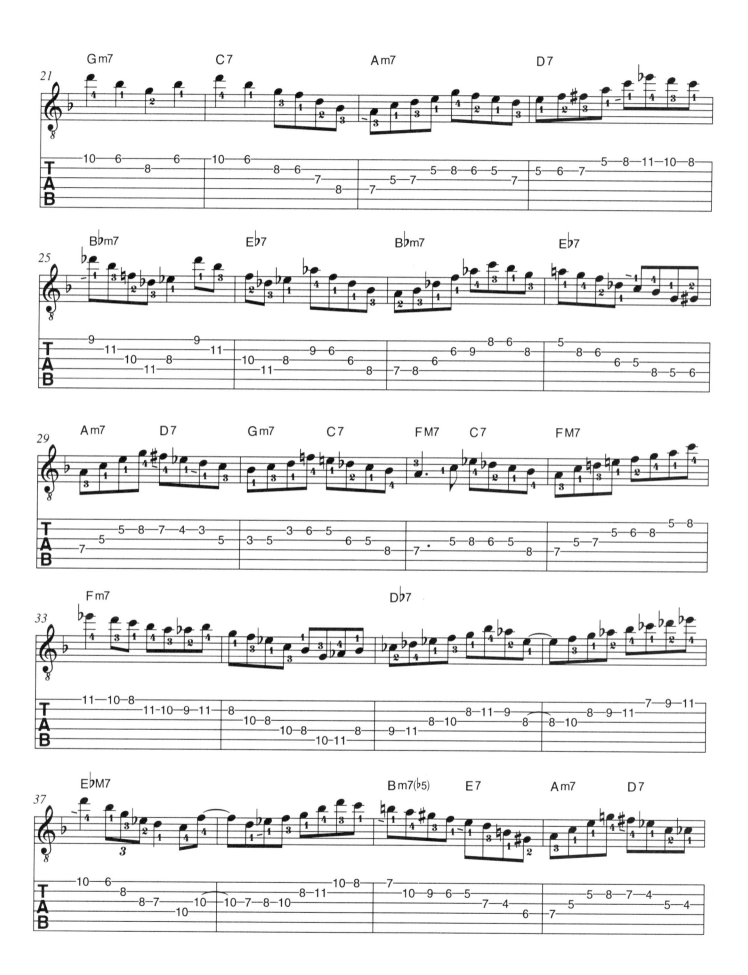

63

STELLA'S MOONLIGHT

Jack Wilkins

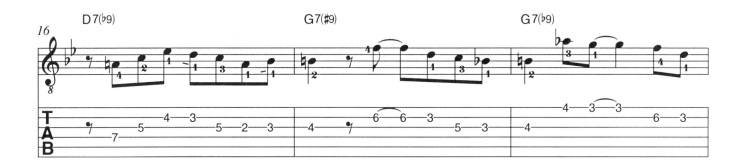

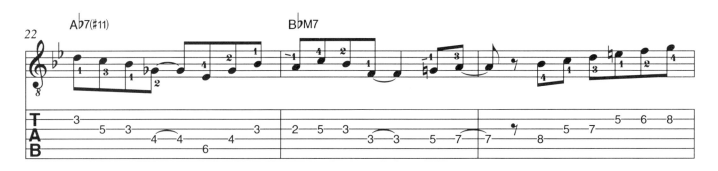

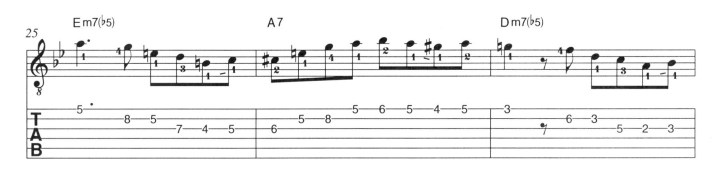

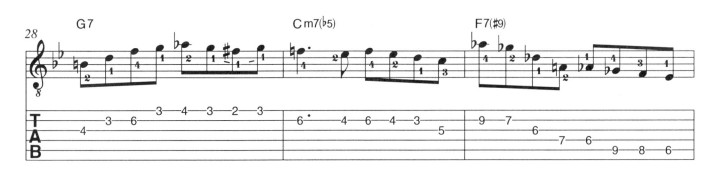

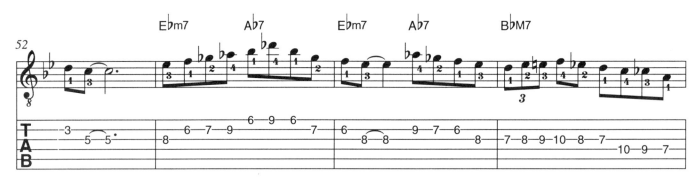

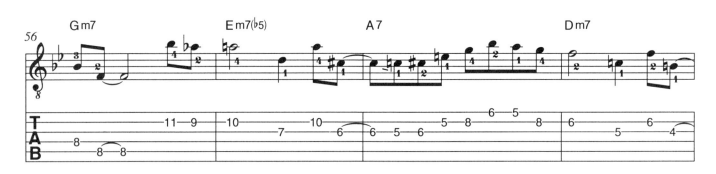

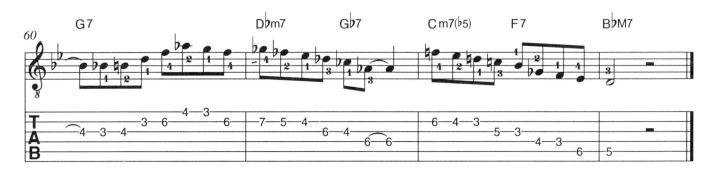

ALL THE THINGS

Jack Wilkins

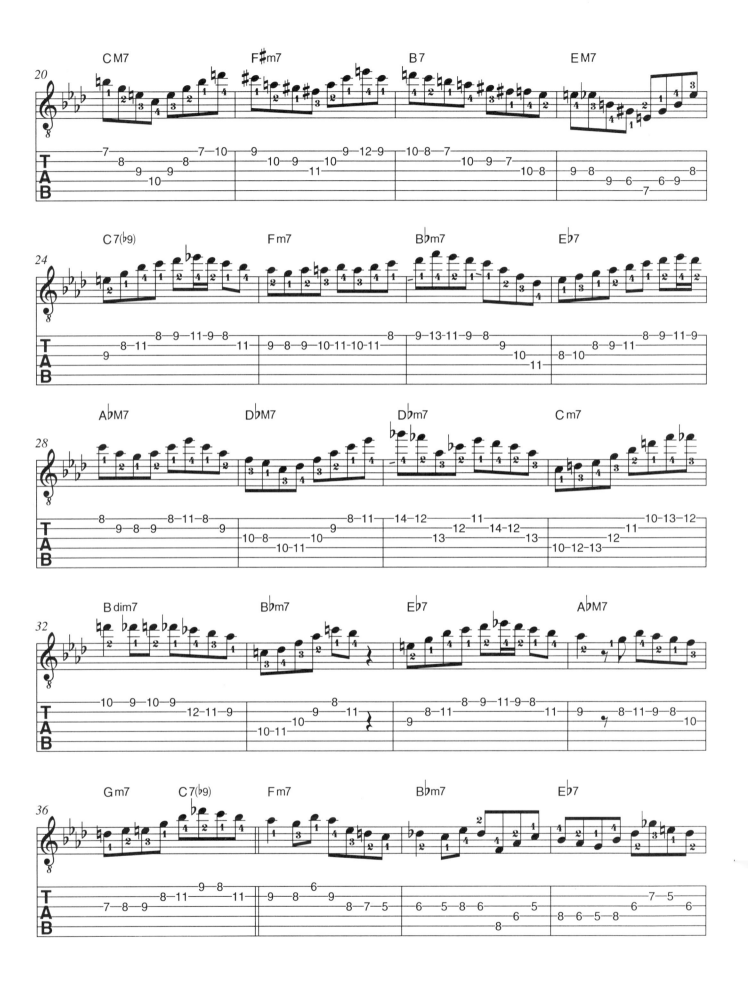

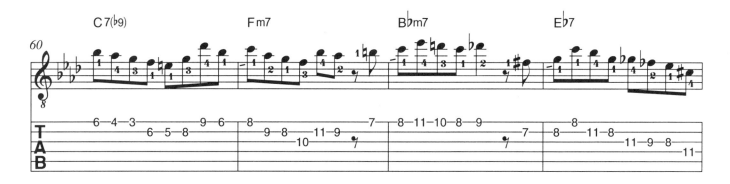

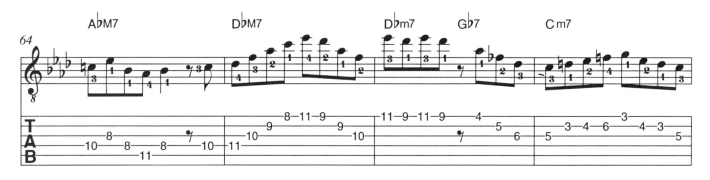

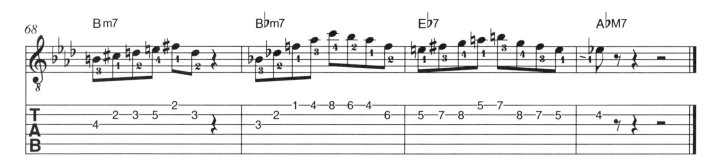

72